Change Here 1 the W(

The story of Bentley Miniature Railway, East Sussex

Early days on *Bentley Miniature Railway* – a passenger 'shuttle' using the 'Uckfield Flyer' in 2-car formation, crossing 'Ridgewood Bridge' prior to the completion of the original circuit. Note the driver's position. April/May 1985.
(J Pollington)

By Tim Sanderson

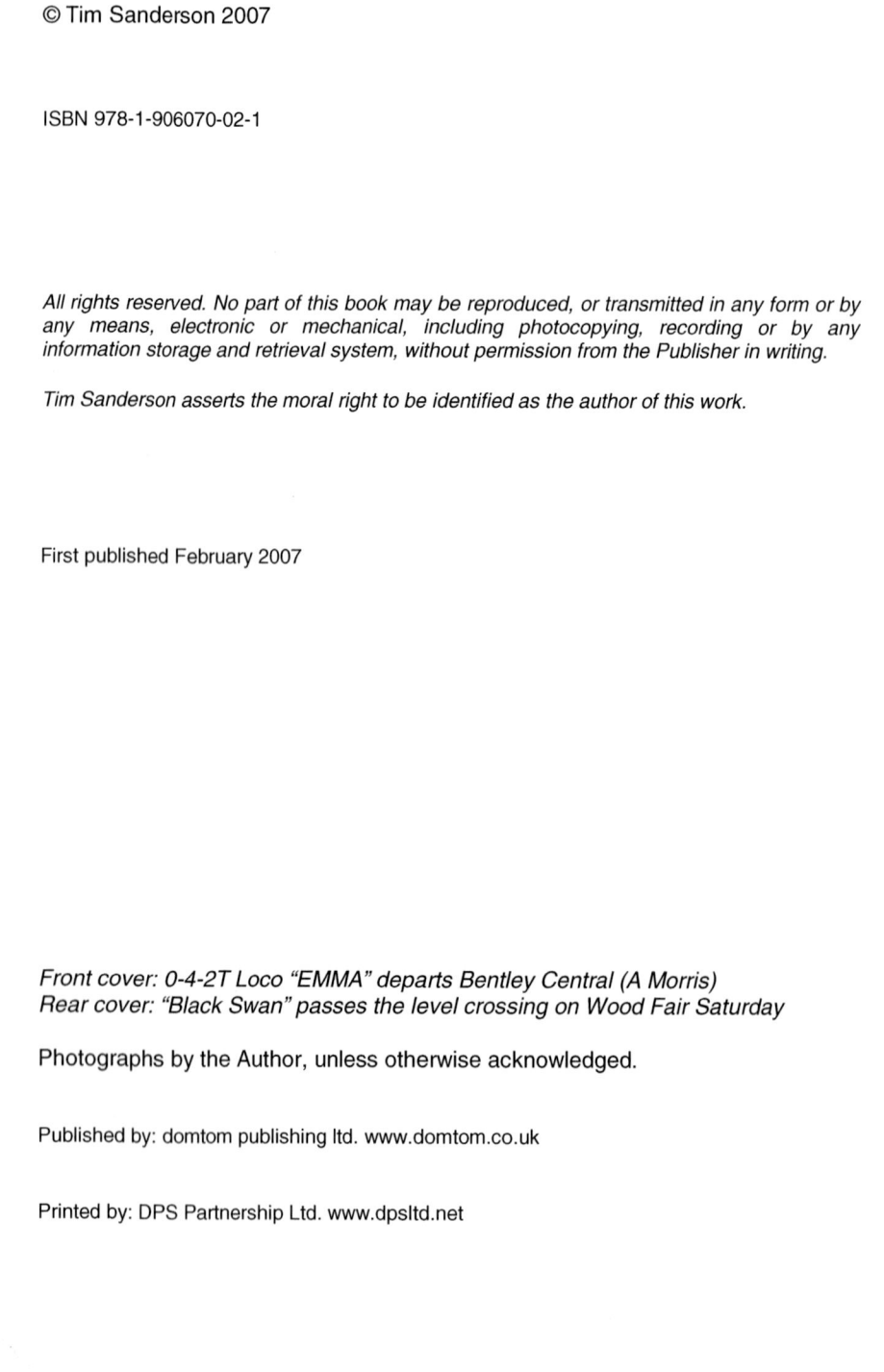

© Tim Sanderson 2007

ISBN 978-1-906070-02-1

All rights reserved. No part of this book may be reproduced, or transmitted in any form or by any means, electronic or mechanical, including photocopying, recording or by any information storage and retrieval system, without permission from the Publisher in writing.

Tim Sanderson asserts the moral right to be identified as the author of this work.

First published February 2007

Front cover: 0-4-2T Loco "EMMA" departs Bentley Central (A Morris)
Rear cover: "Black Swan" passes the level crossing on Wood Fair Saturday

Photographs by the Author, unless otherwise acknowledged.

Published by: domtom publishing ltd. www.domtom.co.uk

Printed by: DPS Partnership Ltd. www.dpsltd.net

Contents

Introduction		ii
Foreword		iv
Chapter One	- Bentley Wildfowl and Motor Museum	1
Chapter Two	- Uckfield Model Railway Club	5
Chapter Three	- Early Days of Bentley Miniature Railway	7
Chapter Four	- The Railway is Developed	13
Chapter Five	- Locomotives and Rolling Stock	19
Chapter Six	- Signalling	27
Chapter Seven	- Trackwork and Civil Engineering	34
Chapter Eight	- A Trip around the Railway	42
Acknowledgements		50
Contacts		50

Drawings

Location Map	1
Bentley Miniature Railway 1985 – 1994	10
Bentley Miniature Railway 1995 – 2007	15
Signalling – Train detection	31
Fig 7.1 Points – Single gauge	37
Fig 7.2 Points – Dual gauge	38

Change here for a Walk in the Woods

Introduction

The year 2006 saw the 21st anniversary of *Bentley Miniature Railway*. Even over these few years, it is inevitable that time dims the memory of events, so, at the beginning of the year, I decided to record the history of this little line.

I joined Uckfield Model Railway Club Ltd, which operates Bentley Miniature Railway via an Operating Committee, in around 1986, so have followed the development of the Railway almost since its beginning. I am grateful, however, to my fellow Club members, for their memories, clarification, and correction of my knowledge. Although produced by agreement, the text of this book does not necessarily represent the opinions of Uckfield Model Railway Club Ltd, Bentley Miniature Railway Operating Committee, or their Officers.

In describing Bentley Miniature Railway, it is perhaps fair to establish what constitutes a **miniature** railway. The definition could be debated endlessly, especially at the boundaries with other types of railway, but, for the purpose of this book, I propose that given below. For those readers who understand the concept, please skip this section, and read on.

In the UK, the national railway system operates on a gauge of 4' 8½" between the rails. This gauge is known as "Standard Gauge". There are many private heritage railways operating on the same gauge. Any railway operating at a gauge less than Standard is known as "Narrow Gauge". Most UK narrow gauge lines are at around 2' to 2' 6" – these would not warrant the description **miniature**. However, both Standard and Narrow Gauge railways could be called "full size".

At the opposite end of the spectrum, a **model** railway would generally be one constructed to replicate a full size railway, whether standard or narrow, real or imaginary, at a particular scale – the common one being "OO" or 4 mm = 1 ft. In a model railway, the trains and track, but importantly the scenery, buildings, etc. are scaled down. Most models would be constructed indoors, on raised boards – however, an increasing number of models are created in the garden, using gauges up to 2½". Although recreating a world in miniature, none of these are miniature railways as such.

So to the essence of a miniature railway. This would generally be constructed on an extra narrow gauge, but with the important requirement, that a person, or people, may travel in or on one or more vehicle(s) hauled by a locomotive. For this purpose, a minimum gauge of 3½" is normal. I propose the maximum gauge for a miniature railway would be 12¼".

A second characteristic is that a miniature railway would generally be used purely for pleasure, rather than to transport humans or goods between two geographically separated places.

Introduction

When it comes to the locomotives, miniature railway locomotives may be constructed to be scale replicas of full size examples, whether steam, diesel, or electrically (battery) operated. Confusion arises when a replica of a Standard Gauge original is operated, on the same miniature gauge, alongside a Narrow Gauge replica. The Standard Gauge replica will appear to be smaller than the Narrow Gauge, although the full size versions would be the opposite – this effect is due to the different scale used. Hence, many miniature railways employ locomotives based on Narrow Gauge prototypes, in order to attain a more powerful locomotive for the given gauge. Going beyond this, there is an increasing tendency for miniature locomotives to be constructed after no particular prototype, but to the largest possible loading gauge for the track gauge. Representatives of all three basic types of locomotive will be found at *Bentley Miniature Railway*.

A miniature railway could be found in a domestic garden, a public park, or other tourist attraction. The first would normally be private, other forms may operate on an occasional, voluntary basis, or as a commercial concern. Miniature railways may have the tracks raised, to enable the passengers to sit astride the coaches (to lower the centre of gravity and aid stability). Other miniature railways are constructed, just like the full size, on the ground with earthworks etc. The simplest miniature railway is straight up and back – as often found at Fetes etc. on a temporary basis. Several take the form of a circle around a feature, such as a lake, often with rudimentary sidings for storage of the motive power and coaches. The more complex railways appear and operate much as a full size, self contained railway might, with full signalling, sidings, loops etc.

Bentley Miniature Railway is: Sited in a Tourist Attraction (Bentley Wildfowl and Motor Museum, East Sussex); operated on a voluntary, non profit basis, by a local Model Railway Club; the track is at ground level, with track gauges of 7¼" and 5" gauntleted; although in reality describing a circuit, the layout is such that this is disguised, and appears to go from one place to another, and return, and is operated as a full size railway. A variety of types of locomotives and coaches may be seen from time to time.

Tim Sanderson
Haywards Heath
January 2007

Change here for a Walk in the Woods

Foreword

Having been a founder member of the Uckfield Model Railway Club in 1973 I have seen the club grow from a few enthusiasts to today's membership of almost 100, whose ages range from teens to eighties and interests vary from the smallest scales i.e.1/148th, to those seen at Bentley.

Tim has been writing articles on many aspects of model railways for several of the monthly and specialist magazines during the past few years, so a logical next step was to write a book. His choice of the subject for this book was of great interest to me as it revives memories of how the Club has developed over the past 30 plus years.

The development could only happen by the many enthusiasts spending many hours designing and building not only the locomotives and rolling stock but the entire infrastructure needed to run a safe and reliable system which we see at Bentley today.

Keith Nock
President, Uckfield Model Railway Club.

CHAPTER ONE

Bentley Wildfowl & Motor Museum

The home of *Bentley Miniature Railway* is known as "Bentley Wildfowl and Motor Museum". This is located near to the towns of Lewes and Uckfield in East Sussex.

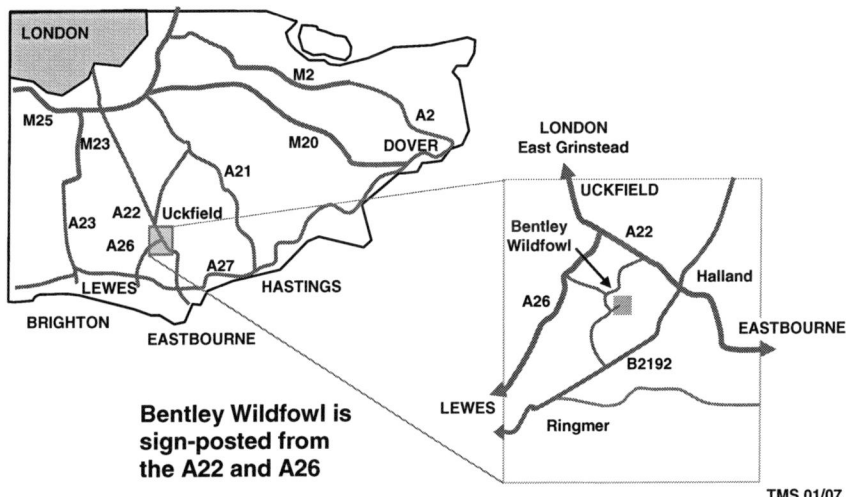

Bentley Wildfowl is sign-posted from the A22 and A26

TMS 01/07

Local to the area is the Glyndebourne Opera at Ringmer; the seaside towns of Brighton, Hastings and Eastbourne, and other attractions are within a day's motoring from the site.

Bentley is recorded as belonging to the Archbishop of Canterbury over 700 years ago. The history of Bentley may be followed up on site.

Bentley House

Gerald and Mary Askew discovered Bentley in 1937. Gerald was keen to take up farming, and developed the landholding after the War. The present estate is very much their creation. Gerald not only farmed, but bred horses, gardened (with the able assistance of Mary) and collected wildfowl.

When the Askews took over, the house itself was old, and unattractively altered. They set about restoration, and sympathetic extension. Additions were made at either end of the existing farm house, consisting of two large Palladian rooms, each with a Palladian window. Inside there is an enfilade along the length of the front. The second, "bird room", was completed in 1968 only shortly before Gerald's death. This room is now dedicated to his memory, and contains Gerald's wildfowl

Change here for a Walk in the Woods

painting collection by Philip Rickman, and a large portrait of Mr Askew feeding his birds.

The Askews' stamp was placed on the interior design, with the use of mid 18th century wallpaper setting the theme of the Chinese room. The bird room at the opposite end contrasts in a restrained and cooler design. The dining room is one of the old rooms with low beams, and contains a 17th century oak farmhouse table, and 18th century Venetian chairs. Decorative, painted furniture is a characteristic of the house.

Formal gardens

In the garden the Askews inherited two lovely species of trees, Ginkgo Biloba and Swamp Cypress which stand in front of the house.

In the formal gardens to the rear, they created a series of 'rooms' with yew hedges as a reflection of the house. The layout is formal but the planning informal. The help and advice of landscape gardener, Jim Russell, was enlisted in this

The Wildfowl Reserve

Gerald Askew's passion was for wildfowl, and the reserve was started by the ordering of twenty pairs of wildfowl from the Wildfowl Trust at Slimbridge. His first thought was where to put these, and the first of a series of lakes was excavated in one of the poorer fields which fortunately uncovered a spring.

Some of the first birds to arrive were Mandarins and Carolinas, Emperor Geese and a pair of Black-necked Swans. This stock was increased and improved by the Askews, and since Gerald's death has been continued to this day.

The reserve has been successful in breeding several species of fowl, including the Ne-ne or Hawaiian Geese, and hundreds of birds have been returned to their original habitat of Hawaii. Although the collection could be self sufficient, in order to improve the breeding stock, and replace birds killed by predators, selected birds are bought in from other collections. Similarly, Bentley stock is passed to other locations.

Although the term wildfowl strictly refers to Swans, Geese and Ducks, visitors to Bentley will also see more exotic species, such as Flamingo and Cranes.

Transfer to East Sussex Council

The Askews' marvellous work was only brought to an end by the death of Gerald Askew in 1970. In 1978, Mary, gave the nucleus of the estate to the people of East Sussex, to be run by East Sussex County Council. Mary continues to live in part of the house to this date (2006).

The Motor Museum

The Council set about adapting the site to provide a tourist attraction. Their first addition was the Motor Museum.

The museum was set up by Hugh Stuart-Roberts who owned many vintage cars and gained enormous pleasure from them until he retired. However, the collection has been loaned by many individual owners who wish them to be more widely seen and enjoyed. They are generally in running order and used on the roads. There is, therefore, a turnover of vehicles available for viewing at any time. Among the events held at Bentley are vehicle rallies, where home and visiting vehicles may be seen running.

Gift Shop and Tea Room

As the visitor enters Bentley, they pass through the Gift Shop, where many items of interest are on sale, including books and souvenirs, many relating to motor vehicles, wildlife and birds, and packets of bird seed. The shop also includes crafts by members of The Sussex Guild whose work provides a wide range of gifts that are ideal for all occasions. For the hungry explorer, the Tea Rooms opposite provide light lunches, sandwiches, drinks and ice creams.

Adjacent to the entrance buildings are the Shire Barn where skilled crafts people demonstrate and sell their work. The Education Block features Woodland and Wildfowl displays, with "hands-on" opportunities to see feel and hear their characteristics. Bentley caters for school parties, and has rooms for this purpose.

Adventure Playground

Just down the hill from the Gift Shop and Tea Rooms, is the Adventure Playground where children up to the age of 10 can let off steam. There is ample space for picnicking in the shade of mature beech and plane trees. Adjacent to this area is the main station, Bentley Central, of *Bentley Miniature Railway*, but this must form the subject of the rest of this book…

Change here for a Walk in the Woods

Glyndebourne Wood

The woodland known as Glyndebourne Wood is accessible by foot from the Adventure Playground, or via *Glyndebourne Wood Halt* of *Bentley Miniature Railway* when it is operating. There is an 800m circular trail through it describing many aspects of woodland management. The whole area is managed as working woodland, a wildlife habitat and a recreational facility.

Glyndebourne Wood includes an "Early Woodworking Centre". Two Anglo-Saxon houses have been reconstructed from local wood. Also in this part of the Wood a Bronze Age house and walkway, a prehistoric bread oven and a 1st century BC kiln for firing pots can be found. Children find this area exciting to investigate at any time of year. However, the wood, and indeed the whole site, come alive during the annual Wood Fair, commenced by the Council, and now continued by the current management.

The Wood Fair is used to demonstrate many techniques for woodland management and uses of wood, including sculptures, which are displayed in the Wood. The Railway too has benefited from the demonstrations during Wood Fair weekend, including a fine hedge laid alongside the main stretch between Bentley Central and Glyndebourne Wood.

There are three simple Orienteering Courses on the Estate. The shortest course takes about 10 minutes to run, and the longest is only 2.0km but can be taken at your leisure. One is wholly within the Wood while a longer one covers both woodland and open land.

New Management

At the end of the 2003 season, having completed some 25 years of running Bentley Wildfowl, East Sussex County Council decided that this operation would no longer fit with their responsibilities to the local community. Therefore, they sought to pass on ownership and operation to another body, more able to develop the site as it deserves.

Following some protracted negotiations throughout 2004, the site was sold back to the Askew family. The, then incumbent managers of the Site and Wildfowl Reserve continue to operate Bentley Wildfowl. Having closed from autumn 2004, Bentley reopened at Easter 2005, and they have continued to develop and publicise the attractions under the new arrangements.

New for 2006 have been a new Model vehicle display, and replanted formal gardens.

CHAPTER TWO

Uckfield Model Railway Club

Birth of the Club

Uckfield Model Railway Club was formed in about 1973. I say "about", as the early records have been lost. First meetings were held in a member's family loft. Here a 10 ft x 8 ft layout in "00" scale (4mm:1 ft on 16.5 mm gauge track) was constructed.

As membership grew, the space available was inadequate; fortunately a member with interests in miniature railways joined, and offered space in the workshop he was building on his property – as long as the Club helped him build it! This served for a few years, but the arrangement was not ideal, and toward the end of the 1970's, the opportunity arose to take over a redundant building on the former Army Camp, at Maresfield, just outside Uckfield. The Club members renovated and installed power here, to make it fit to work in. When the Council wanted to demolish the building, the Club was offered space in a new Gymnasium on the same site. This had all mod cons, including central heating, and toilets available. The Club moved in approximately 1980. At these two locations, the first Club layout that could be erected permanently was built – 'Maresfield to Duddleswell', again in "00". This was developed to become a circular arrangement. In order to take this layout to exhibitions, a trailer was constructed on a redundant caravan chassis. This became known as the "Wendy House". The arrangement of moving the large layout (which was heavy due to its construction in ¾" chipboard!) was not satisfactory, so from about 1986, a new exhibition layout, using modular baseboards of plywood open frame construction, was commenced. In EM (still 4mm:1 ft, but on 18.2 mm gauge) the model was named Treyarnon. This was easily transported in the back of members' vehicles. The "Wendy House" was therefore pensioned off to Bentley. 'Maresfield to Duddleswell' became a Clubroom layout, and saw much use for running members' stock.

As described in the next Chapter, the Club soon gathered members with an interest in live steam. This lead to the construction of the portable track, and this is still, very much, a part of the Club, and is used regularly, particularly at an annual modelling exhibition in Brighton, during February.

Growth of UMRC

The Club started to run our own Model Railway Exhibition in 1975, through a joint show with another Club, at a local Garden Centre. From 1976 to 1985, an Exhibition was held annually, initially in an outbuilding of a local hostelry, then in the Uckfield Public Hall. When it became no longer possible to use this Hall, our own Exhibition terminated. We then supported other Clubs with their exhibitions. However, the opening of a brand new Civic Hall in Uckfield allowed an Exhibition

Change here for a Walk in the Woods

in 1992, leading to the annual Uckfield Model Railway Club Exhibition, in October each year, commencing in 1996. This has become a great success, and is eagerly awaited by Enthusiasts.

By the late 1980's, the Maresfield building had been sold off to the Gymnastics Club, the main occupiers. Although relations were good, it was clear that we did not fit in with their use of the building. Therefore, UMRC terminated our rental, and started to look for premises where we could develop our own way. Sadly, 'Maresfield to Duddleswell' had to be dismantled. While we looked for premises, we returned to meeting in members' homes. Over the next 3 – 4 years, we actually managed to construct a layout in "O" scale (7mm:1 ft) 32 ft long, in a member's garage. Baseboards were once again modular plywood, a design which has served well for all Club layouts since. In order to assemble the whole layout for testing prior to its first outing, a room at Bentley Wildfowl and Motor Museum was hired for two weeks.

During these events, the search for a permanent home for the Modelling interests was continuing. This bore fruit during 1993, and the Club signed a lease on a redundant 2-storey building behind a shop in Uckfield High Street. We entered the premises in the autumn, and, once again, set about installing power, lighting and all the little conveniences we hoped for (except the "Conveniences" themselves!). The stable use of our own premises has permitted the modellers to construct several new layouts. These have visited many exhibitions, flying the flag for the Club, and earned well deserved commendations.

With such diverse interests, inevitably some members will champion one or other discipline. However mostly we work together for Club events, and, as will be described later, peak day operations at Bentley Miniature Railway are supported by Modellers, who, like the Author, sometimes become hooked, and merge their allegiances!

The Club was formed into a Limited Company, in 1998.

What goes around comes around, and in 2006 the premises with which our building was associated came up for redevelopment. The Club decided that, rather than sit out the remaining terms of our lease, we would find new premises once more. The search was a little shorter than the previous time, and in September 2006, we took over a single storey industrial unit, only a few hundred metres from the Maresfield Gymnasium and across the A22 Maresfield bypass! This has again been fitted out for our use, and we hope we can remain for many more years.

CHAPTER THREE

Early Days of Bentley Miniature Railway

Portable Track – the origins of Bentley Miniature Railway

The member whose workshop the Club helped to construct introduced other like minded people, who were keen on operating 7¼" gauge live steam railways. Together, interested parties assembled a portable ground level track and this was put to use at Exhibitions, Fetes and the like, raising money for Club funds. From these beginnings, the yearnings to operate a proper, permanent miniature railway grew into the subject of the rest of this book. To run on this, a 2 or 3-car replica of the diesel multiple unit trains, running on the main line from London to Uckfield, was constructed. Named the "Uckfield Flyer" this was powered by a succession of lawnmower engines, driving via bicycle chain to one bogie. Steam traction was provided by members' locomotives, hauling sit-astride bogie coaches, which had simple timber and hardboard bodies.

Beginnings

Having commenced with the Motor Museum, around 1982 East Sussex County Council planned for a miniature railway in the grounds of Bentley Wildfowl. They entered negotiations with one local Society, which later broke down and, as Uckfield Model Railway Club had been looking for such a site, we stepped in. The then Club president negotiated with the Council for something like nine months before an agreement was signed in May 1984.

As the Club had been running passenger hauling miniature trains for some years, using the portable track, and early stock, the opportunity to, at last, develop a permanent Miniature Railway was met with enthusiasm by members. Even whilst construction was commenced, the portable track was laid in a circle within the future circuit, to provide rides during 1984.

Work started immediately after the Agreement was signed; the Club was contracted to run in 10½ months! By mid-October the earthworks were completed, which included two culvert bridges over a ditch or small stream.

The terms "Bentley Wildfowl and Motor Museum" and "Bentley Miniature Railway" are quite a mouthful. As a consequence, Club members tend to say "Bentley" to mean either! The context usually determines which is meant. In this book, for short reference I use the term "Bentley" to mean the whole site, and "the Railway" or "BMR" to mean Bentley Miniature Railway.

Change here for a Walk in the Woods

Completion of the track, May 1985 – Bentley House behind

The first passenger train around the permanent circuit - "Uckfield Flyer" leaving
the bare Bentley Central Station, early May Bank Holiday 1985
(Both - J Pollington)

The Layout

The layout as built was limited by the lack of funds in the first instance. The main line was a circuit of approximately 600ft with a station loop branched off it of approximately 200ft. Putting the platform directly behind the children's play area gives them ready access to the trains, yet they were kept well clear of the 'main line' with it being in the next field. The Club opted for three gauges, 3½, 5, and 7¼" laid at ground level. Sixty foot minimum radius curves and a 1 in 100 max

Early Days of Bentley Miniature Railway

gradient were followed. The intention was to enable the 3½" locomotives to be able to do some hauling too. The station loop was kept level throughout.

Construction

The ground in Bentley is predominately of clay, leading to a bog in wet weather, and iron in the summer! In view of these soggy ground conditions, drainage was arranged from the track foundations to the ditch, by buried pipe, or excavated channels. The earthworks were left to settle for the winter while the members switched their attentions to track construction. Steel was chosen in preference to aluminium rail. We opted for German rolled steel flat bottom rail section of 1kg per metre. We used No.8 x ¾" countersunk Phillips head screws with ¼"/M6 large flat washers to hold the rail down to softwood sleepers soaked in creosote. Lengths were prefabricated in a large shed. The work was completed and the track laid (5" and 7¼" only) ballasted and tamped, in time for May Day Bank Holiday. The opportunity was taken to gain experience over the two May bank holidays, before the opening on 2nd June 1985.

The opening was carried out by the comedian, Ken Goodwin, who drove a locomotive of the 'Romulus' type through the ceremonial tape, at the head of a cavalcade of members' and friends' locomotives.

Operation

Initial operation was Sundays and Bank Holidays only from June to August. This was soon extended to include Easter to May, and September. Since the early '90s the Railway has also run on Saturday afternoons during the season and on Wednesdays during August (plus the first Wednesday in September where this immediately followed the August Bank Holiday) although not contracted to do so.

In these first years, the normal run consisted of three clockwise circuits of the track, twice bypassing the station via the main line, and return to the station. Passengers disembark at the steaming bay end of the platform, while a second train may load at the other end.

Developments

After the first season, the 3½" gauge rail was laid in to the circuit. The stated intentions from the beginning were to have a station building, signal box and signalling, and steaming bays with turntable and loading ramp. In these early years, stock was unloaded from members' vehicles on the level crossing at the rear of the circuit. The ramp was therefore a priority, and was installed during 1987/8. A triple gauge turntable, with all the complications of switching the 3½" and 5" tracks to maintain their offsets, was installed in a concreted well. The table is 13ft long, and runs on a 4ft diameter ball race. The table ends rest, and run, on

Change here for a Walk in the Woods

steel plates for support at each bay position. Individual bays, of single gauge, a connection to the main line, and a multi-gauge ramp to the grass car parking/loading area were installed. Many locomotives are brought each time by their owner/drivers, and offloaded down the ramp from the parking area.

The Station building followed in 1989. Brick built, it includes two ticket windows, and provides a congregation area for staff, and shelter from the elements. The signal box was built in 1991. Also of brick, with all-round windows for visibility, the signalling system has been extended from here since the box was finished.

By 1990, it was evident that the 3½" gauge was not viable, and all further additions have catered for 5" and 7¼" gauges only. The fourth rail for the 3½" was slowly recovered for reuse, and the last length disappeared about 1992 (except for the remaining original turnouts, which still feature the extra rail with the complications of addition crossings).

Initially, rolling stock, most of which belongs to the Club, was stored "off-track" in the Wendy House shed. The need for a tracked storage area was soon realised, and planning permission sought for in the south west corner of the site. This was granted in 1991. The storage was completed in 1992, and has five roads fed via 5-way stub points, in 7¼" only.

For several years the Railway was know as *Bentleyrail*, but this title was abandoned in favour of the conventional name. The change was made between 1995 and 1996 seasons.

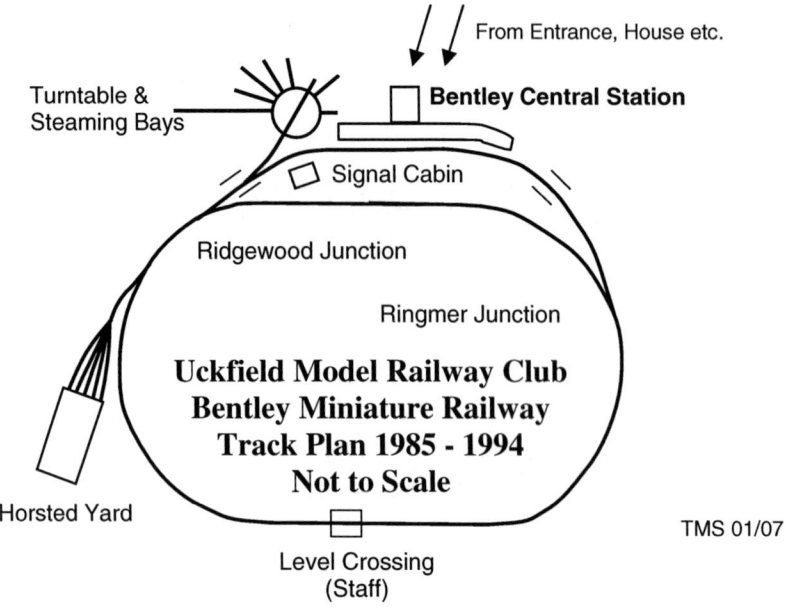

TMS 01/07

Bentley House 2006

The portable track in use at Bentley, during construction of the permanent track.

Bentley Central Platform approach
Top: August 1985 (J Pollington)
Bottom: September 2006

CHAPTER FOUR

The Railway is Developed
1995 to 2006

The Extension

It had always been the intention to extend the railway. Plans and surveys were carried out with the idea of extending into the nearby Glyndebourne Wood, with a generous balloon loop. Bentley management were very supportive, and a final plan was submitted for us, by Bentley, to the local planning authority. The initial desire to enter the woods was opposed by those who believe that woodland and railways do not mix! However, by shortening the run up to the woods, and completing the loop outside the woodland proper, permission was granted in 1993. In faith that permission would be forthcoming, the entry and exit points for the extension were fabricated, and installed prior to obtaining permission. A bridge over the pond by the start of the extension was completed, and some track (in the original style) was laid out to cross the bridge and beyond.

Work started to excavate the ground. The loop was to be in a cutting, and the gradients were chosen to use the spoil removed to build the embankment that brings the line from Bentley Central Station towards the woods at first on the level, then a gentle climb, in a straight line.

The work was carried out by Club members, using a dumper truck, which was purchased, and a JCB excavator and driver hired through a member. Once the route had been surveyed and marked out, the cutting was pulled out by the excavator, and the spoil piled in the centre of the loop. In this way, the use of the excavator was limited. We then had the task of transferring the earth to its final position. This was done by hand and the dumper.

Whilst the earthworks were in progress, the track materials were obtained. After experience with the original rail section, a larger section was chosen - medium steel rail, at 3.76 lb/yard (1.87 kg/m) and in nominal 4 m lengths. This was to be laid on softwood timbers (2" x 2" x 15"). Fixing was by large headed self-tapping screws. Since the first part of the Railway was constructed, the Club had obtained permanent headquarters in Uckfield. Fabrication of track panels was commenced at the headquarters. The sleepers were cut, drilled, and soaked in creosote - much to the chagrin of the 'modelling' side of the membership.

Once the rail was delivered, two "converter" tracks were completed, from the old, light rail section, to the heavier. We now commenced track panel assembly in earnest. As panels were completed, we transported them to site, and began laying them out, to check that we had the right quantity of each type. All this took through 1994, and early 1995. By Easter '95, it was clear that, with a following wind, we would have the circuit connected by May/June. A low-key opening was planned for the first weekend in June. This coincided with the tenth anniversary of the opening

Change here for a Walk in the Woods

of Bentley Miniature Railway, and (approximately) the twenty first year of the club. In fact, the track was ready for trains by the Spring Bank Holiday weekend, and some trains were run unofficially then. A mass turnout of members was requested for the week between the Bank Holiday and opening weekend. Much tidying up was carried out, although perhaps it was a case of sweeping things under the carpet! The route was measured by wheel, and came to 772 metres from Bentley Central via the extension and straight back into the station. See the drawing opposite for the final track plan

The opening weekend started damp and cold, although the weekend cleared a little for the members' barbecue on the Saturday evening. A few drivers braved the elements to mark the occasion by driving round in cavalcade. By contrast, the rest of the summer was hot and hotter, and by the end, we could hardly get a spade into the ground to continue with grading and tidying the site!

For the 1995 season, neither the station nor the loop at Glyndebourne Wood were commissioned. The points for the loop were constructed during winter 1995-6. The tunnel was also completed by roofing over the cutting at that point. The portals were constructed from brick arches, whilst breeze blocks form the internal walls, supporting corrugated iron rings for roofing. Once finished, the ground was reinstated over the roof, thus providing access to the centre of the loop. The tunnel is about 6' high in the centre, and wide enough to allow passengers to disembark either side, should there be any reason (not that there has been any emergency in the history of the Railway).

Consolidation

Once the basic trackwork was completed, work continued to tidy up the site. The signal box, platform name boards, etc. were erected at Glyndebourne Wood. With the commissioning of the signal box, the signalling system was extended and refined. Full details of Signalling are given in Chapter 6.

Although basic fencing had been applied around the new route to protect the public from the trains, some additional screening was required. Along the outside of the main straight double track, hedges were planted. Over the course of several "Wood Fair" weekends, the art of hedge laying was demonstrated on the growing plants, resulting in the present fine hedge screening the track from view. Similarly, trees were planted, both by the Club and by Bentley management, in the middle of the Glyndebourne cutting area, and opposite Glyndebourne platform – thus creating a woodland effect around the line denied by the inability to enter the wood itself.

Landscaping has been carried out, mainly grass areas either side of the tracks. The area in the middle of the original circuit is mainly grass, with several trees. During busy summer weekends, staff members may be found camping or caravanning in this area, providing overnight attention and early opening of the Railway.

The Railway is Developed

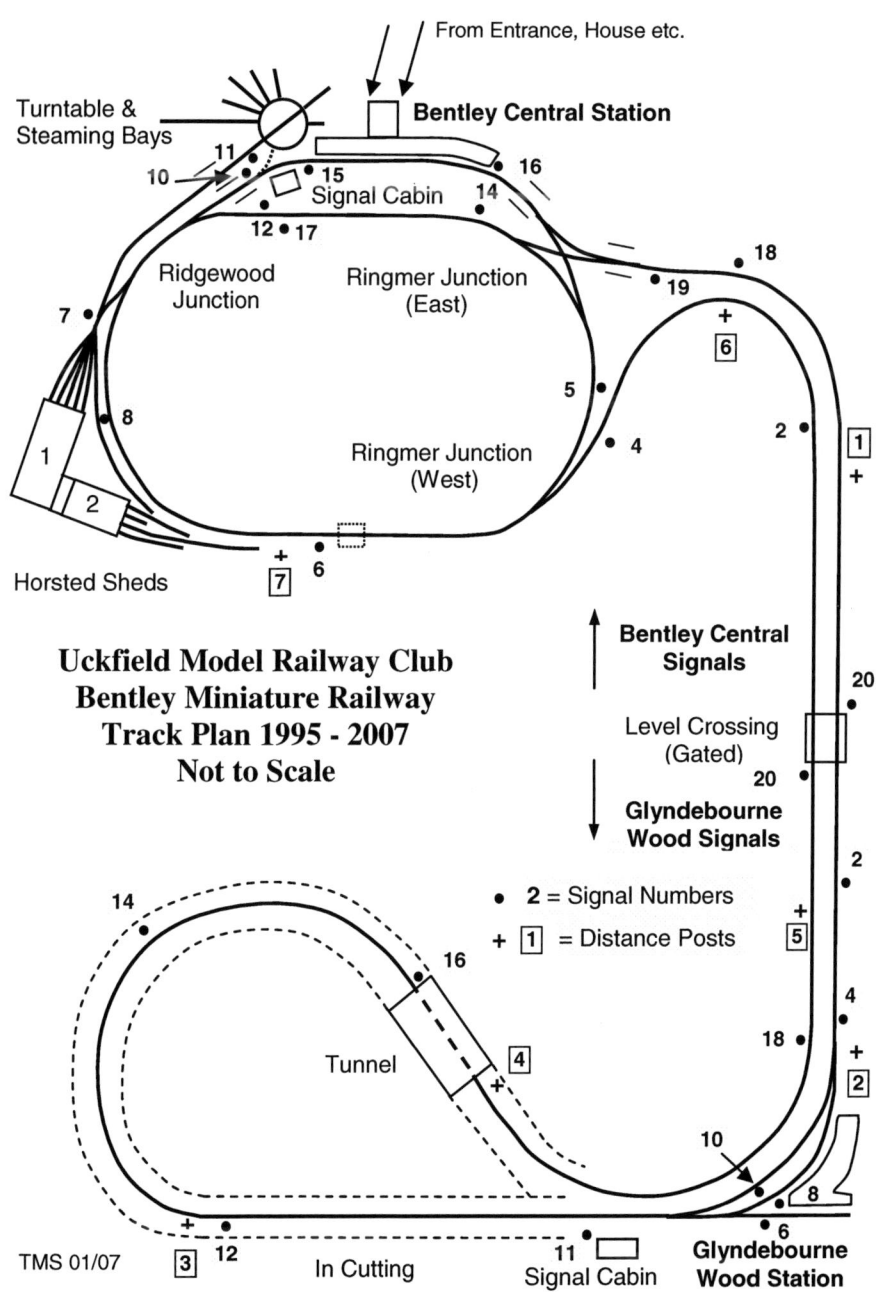

Change here for a Walk in the Woods

Trees have also been placed on the inside of the return curve into the Bentley Central area. The field on this side of the line has become known as "Railway Field" and is generally used for grazing sheep or cattle; however, this also forms the events field for special events, when public access from the main area to the field has to be provided across the level crossing, staff for this being provided by the Railway.

Buildings

The initial station building and signal box at Bentley Central were constructed in brick, with slate roofs. The station building provides ticket office, mess area, and general gathering area, and is 10 ft long and 6 ft wide. On arrival at the Railway staff sign-in to the day's book here, for insurance purposes. The building was originally entered from the Park end via a wooden door; however, this was inconvenient for staff, and the layout was altered to include a door from the platform, which is now used exclusively for access. There are two opening ticket windows on the side facing the departure platform, although one has always been sufficient, and the second is now used to display a board announcing when the Railway is next operating. On the arrival side of the building are two similar, but fixed, windows. These give light to the sink and fridge area.

When the first rolling stock shed was constructed, this was a low building, for small coaches and locos only. This was constructed from breeze block, with corrugated cement roofing material. After some years of use, the roof was raised to allow personnel entrance – although still not at full height, so heads must be watched! No windows are installed, but the front is shut off by secure doors. Additions have since been made, either side, to give general storage for tools, gardening equipment, etc. The extension to the right has recently been converted to a further carriage storage area, with lower headroom, and including, for the first time, 5" gauge tracks.

From the earliest days, the "Wendy House" from the modelling side of the Club was sited to the left of the carriage shed. This was used for storage of materials. As the Railway expanded, more and more stock came to the line, and tended to remain for the season. Permission was therefore obtained to erect a second stock shed. This was to become known as "Horsted Yard 2", the original shed being "Horsted Yard 1". In order to erect this new shed, the Wendy House was demolished. The final development of the two sheds includes a workshop/storage area between the two stock sheds.

As the plan of the railway (page 15) shows, Horsted Yard 2 building is at right angles to Shed 1, with the entrance away from the original shed. The new shed has similar breeze block walls at the rear and blank end, but the side facing the public is faced in brick, with arched blank window openings. Originally, access to Horsted 2 was planned by facing points from the main line, as it climbs

The Railway is Developed

at the rear of the circuit. The disadvantages of this, and the realisation that an access track could be squeezed between the corner of the new shed, and the main line, if this latter was realigned slightly, led to the arrangement that brings a line from "layover" points at the entrance to Horsted 1, to a headshunt in front of No 2. The tracks into this shed are fed by two further "layover" points (see Chapter 7).

The "standard" colour of buildings is Buckingham Green (doors mostly) with White and/or Cream frames, etc. to offset.

Lineside furniture

The character of any railway is augmented by the little items to be seen beside the track. *Bentley Miniature Railway* is no exception. Wooden signs advising passengers that they have arrived at a Station; to 'Wait until the train has stopped' or to 'Sit Upright' have been painted by members in the house colours of Green background with White lettering. Other signs instructing drivers where to sound a warning - "SW" boards – or, temporarily, to reduce speed – "C" and "T" boards – may be observed around the line. As well as the arm on the signpost erected by Bentley Wildfowl, directing visitors to the Children's playground and Railway, when the Railway is operating we temporarily place a folding sign board board at the top of the path leading to Bentley Central Station.

Once the railway had reached its current extent, the distance from Bentley Central was measured, and distance posts placed every 100 metres. These show simply a single figure to denote number of 100's. At the same time, gradient boards were constructed to mark the change between Level and Up or Down, or between gradients. These all were initially constructed from wood, with adhesive lettering. However, they did not last long, and the current set has been assembled from plastic sheet background, painted white, and with individual numbers/letters screwed in place – 3" high brass numbers for distance posts, and 1½" plastic characters for gradients. These are mounted on 2" plastic downpipe, using matching brackets.

Early in the development of BMR, a full size gradient post and mile post were obtained from British Rail and mounted beside the track. Although not giving true figures, these add to the authenticity of the Railway.

Operation

The Club's original licence to operate the Railway required us to run on Sundays and Bank Holidays during the Easter to September season. These are still our busiest days, and, weather permitting, several locomotives may be seen operating. However, for our own enjoyment, Saturday afternoons, and Wednesdays during the School Summer Holidays were soon added. As the Railway grew, further days were added around the Bank Holidays. When the new

Change here for a Walk in the Woods

Management took over Bentley, they requested that we run more days, and from 2004, the Railway is open every day of School Holidays and every Saturday and Sunday from Easter to the end of September, plus October Half Term. Since staff are normally on site for maintenance work on Winter Sundays, if any passengers present themselves, a train (usually the Tram) can be operated at short notice.

The Present

When East Sussex Council decided to close Bentley, it was an anxious time for the Club and BMR. Through 2004, we carried on operations, and maintained the line as necessary. However plans for development were put on hold. By the end of that season, when Bentley closed to the public (previously there had been limited winter opening) there were hopes for the future of the site, and we were permitted on site over the winter to continue maintenance. Once the new ownership and management were in place, we were able to prepare the Railway for the 2005 Season, which opened at Easter. During negotiations between ESCC and interested parties, some grand schemes were mooted, which may have led to the Railway growing out of recognition. However, the current Management have, perhaps, more realistic horizons. The Club were persuaded to operate the Railway more frequently, as described above. This has stretched the resources of the membership, particularly during the mid-week operations, but fortunately several members are retired or self-employed (the Author included) and a core of dedicated 'midweekers' has developed. Several of these are members who would consider themselves as modellers, rather than engineers; many modellers also join the ranks for Wood Fair and other busy weekends.

Now that the future of Bentley is more or less secure, ideas for improving the Railway have been floated. The current track relaying around the original circuit is recognised as a priority. However, there have long been plans to take the Railway into, or up to the Wildfowl Reserve itself. These are supported by Bentley Management and informal surveys and discussions have taken place. One possibility would be to diverge from the outward route, after signal BC18, and carry on straight across the site, to a Station near the Wildfowl entrance, turning right to follow the outer fence of the Reserve, before turning right again, and returning to Glyndebourne Wood, entering that Station along the current Bay platform line. The Author hopes that, once the track renewal is complete, and finance is made available, firm plans can be made. However, as this book was completed, another possibility has arisen; whatever transpires, *Bentley Miniature Railway* will not remain static!

CHAPTER FIVE

Locomotives and Rolling Stock

As mentioned in the Introduction, miniature railway locomotives may not always be models of full size ones. The locomotives at Bentley are of three main types:

    a. Scale models of Standard Gauge prototypes
    b. Scale models of, or based on Narrow Gauge prototypes
    c. Heavy haulers, designed for the miniature gauge.

Within these types, propulsion may be Steam, Electric (battery on board), or Internal Combustion.

Most locomotives belong to members, and are brought to site as required; however a number of notable visitors have appeared and these are included below in the listings. Whilst certain locos have their own tender, others use one of the Club's or a dedicated driving truck for the driver to sit on, and operate. These often also contain the coal and water supplies for the steam locos.

Scale Standard Gauge Models

Name	Type	Built	Gauge	Scale
HERCULES	0-4-0 Saddle Tank. Steam	Unknown	7¼"	One eighth
HERCULES is our Club steam loco. This little 0-4-0 saddle-tank is regularly in steam during the summer months, and occasionally performs on our portable track. Compared to the standard 'Hercules' design, this engine has a longer than normal boiler with a larger firebox. It has been operating regularly in 2006.				
Hymecs	Bo-Bo. Battery Electric	2005 2005	7¼" 5"	One eighth 1/11
Bentley Miniature Railway was used as the testing ground for the prototype. The Club purchased this Beyer Peacock Hymek Bo-Bo loco in 2005, which is now a regular club loco at Bentley, and saw its first portable track event in February 2006. A second 5" version from the same Manufacturer has now joined the Club's loco.				
LORNA	2-4-0 Tender. Steam	1990	7¼"	One eighth
LORNA is named after the owner and builder's wife and is a model of a Great Central Railway (Ex-M.S. & L.) Sacre-designed 2-4-0 Class 12A.				

Change here for a Walk in the Woods

Name	Type	Built	Gauge	Scale
Black 5	4-6-0 Tender. Steam	late 1980's	7¼"	One eighth

This 'Black 5' 4-6-0 loco based upon the design of a very popular L.M.S. main line passenger-carrying locomotive has done much service, and has certainly proven that it can pull large trains with ease. This loco was rarely seen at Bentley between 2003/4 due to a major overhaul which has now been completed. The loco returned to service late in 2005 and ran daily during Wood Fair with high passenger volumes and has since run regularly during 2006.

Buffalo	2-8-0 Tender. Steam	1982	7¼"	One eighth

This 2-8-0 loco used to be a regular visitor to the railway all the way from Scotland, but as its owner has now moved back south, it has become one of our most frequent steamers. It is based upon a Canadian National Railway prototype, and as befits a loco from Canada, it has been seen pulling every coach the club possesses with ease for hours on end. This loco has recently undergone major works to change all the wheels tyres which had gradually distorted out of true, but we are glad to welcome it back now and you can expect to see it regularly.

Cindy	0-4-2 Tank. Steam	1994	7¼"	One eighth

This 0-4-2 configuration pannier tank loco was a new addition for 2005 and despite its small size we hope to see it regularly pulling a number of passengers or a rake of wagons on the quieter running days such as Saturdays.

Dart	0-4-2 Tank. Steam	c1986 & 2003	7¼"	One eighth

Bentley plays host to two GWR 'Dart's', both numbered 1466, the first of which took part in the 1999 **S**even and a **Q**uarter **L**ocomotive **E**fficiency **C**ompetition (**SEQLEC**) hosted at Bentley, sponsored by the Model Engineer magazine, and proudly returned home in third position. During the summer, particularly midweek, this loco can often be seen running at Bentley. The second 'Dart' is a more recent addition only being completed during the 2003 running season, but has regularly been seen running on Summer Saturdays since.

Flying Scotsman	4-6-2 Tender	1950's	7¼"	One eighth

This magnificent engine is often rostered to haul passenger trains on our very busiest weekends. It is an accurate model of the L.N.E.R. A3 Pacific (4-6-2) express engine No.4472 and was built almost 50 years ago.

Locomotives and Rolling Stock

Name	Type	Built	Gauge	Scale
Class 73	Bo-Bo Battery Electric	1986	7¼"	One eighth
This loco has had a long history at Bentley starting out as a genuinely petrol-powered loco. After a major internal rebuild it has been converted to purely battery electric operation. The extra space generated by the removal of the petrol engine made room for 4 heavy duty batteries which were proven durable during the construction of the extension in 1994/95 and it is now often seen pulling public at bank holidays.				
Class 31	Co-Co. Battery Electric	2004	7¼"	One eighth
At Bentley we play host to two Class 31 locos. The first has become a regular visitor to Bentley since the 2004 season. The second is an occasional visitor. A powerful battery-electric loco, with space for super-large batteries in the case of the latter, under the lightweight glass-fibre body. This is one of many designs which are commercially available as ready-to-run models, and is based upon the ubiquitous Brush Type 2 diesels seen for many years on the main lines.				
Dock Shunter	4-wheel Battery Electric	2004 2006	7¼" 5"	One eighth 1/11
These are based on small standard gauge dock shunters. "Jenny" in 7¼" gauge is often seen running for the public at BMR, especially on busy days or Saturdays, and is a regular attendee at portable track events. Her smaller sister often rounds off a day of running whilst the steam engines are being cleaned down and can easily haul a full carriage of adults.				
Western Talisman	Co-Co Battery Electric		5"	1/11
This scale model of Class 52 Western locomotive number D1007 is named Western Talisman and is regularly seen on Saturday afternoons.				

Scale Narrow Gauge Models

Name	Type	Built	Gauge	Scale
BASIL	0-4-0 Saddle Tank Freelance Bagnall type.	Unknown	7¼"	Approx One Third
This loco was first run in 2004 and is a 0-4-0 saddle tank Bagnall design loco. It has since become one of the regular operators at the track.				

Change here for a Walk in the Woods

Name	Type	Built	Gauge	Scale
Sweet William	0-4-0 Saddle Tank	Unknown	7¼"	Not Applicable
We have had a number of Sweet Williams at Bentley. Two engines are from the same stable, although they look entirely different! 'WILLIAM I' has a square-topped saddle tank, and 'WILLIAM II' is a tender loco. Both are based upon the 7¼" gauge version of the popular 5" gauge 'Sweet Pea' design. Due to running and boiler problems neither of these locos operated passenger services during 2005. William II has since been run several times in 2006.				
ELAINE, JASMINE, LADY JOY	0-4-0 Saddle Tank + Tender Quarry Hunslet	1997 c1997 1985	7¼"	One Third
Each portrays a 1/3rd scale model of an 0-4-0 saddle-tank Hunslet so typical of those which operated in the old Welsh slate quarries. Each of these is in service regularly at Bentley. Each has their own characteristics; ELAINE and JASMINE are of 'Alice' class with plain boilers, LADY JOY is of 'later Port Dinorwic' type with domed boiler. ELAINE has no tender, and is cab-less, the others have cabs.				
TAURUS, REMUS, ROMULUS (x 2), RHIAN	0-4-0 well tank Freelance design	Various	7¼"	Not Applicable
Five of this popular class of locomotive have operated at BMR. They are built to the popular 'Romulus' design, and have a 0-4-0 wheel arrangement. REMUS has been steaming with Uckfield MRC on its portable track at fetes and fairs long before the railway at Bentley was built. Unusually for the class, REMUS has a round-topped steam dome cover (formed from part of a diver's old air cylinder!) but is otherwise faithful to the original design, complete with well-tank between the frames. TAURUS has been running at Bentley for the last ten years, and has operated with a number of different tenders over that time. ROMULUS has a large 6-wheeled tender and has recently undergone major work to the boiler. ROMULUS (2) first ran for the public at BMR in 2001. ROMULUS (2) is also unusual in that it has an open cab. RHIAN is the most recent addition being completed in 2006. The Romulus's have proven themselves to be a truly 'mixed-traffic' loco over the years, hauling many goods trains during the engineering works on the extension of the line to Glyndebourne Wood, as well as the more usual passenger services which they can regularly be seen undertaking with pleasure.				
Sweet Pea	0-4-0 Saddle Tank	Unknown	5"	Not Applicable
Sweet Pea is a 5" narrow gauge loco which is now seldom seen at Bentley, but was one of the earliest locos to run after the current track was laid.				

The Club's Hymec locomotive leaves Bentley Central for Glyndebourne Wood, with a typical full train
(A Morris)

A study in concentration – the Author negotiates his Narrow Gauge Hunslet "LADY JOY" over the points of Ridgewood Junction, approaching Bentley Central.
(A. Morris)

The Tram LADY HELEN rounds the corner from Bentley Central toward the long straight

Battery Electric "Western" loco with one of the early sit-astride coaches
(A Morris)

Locomotives and Rolling Stock

Name	Type	Built	Gauge	Scale
Tom Rolt	0-4-2 Tank	2001	5"	One Fifth

Based on the Talyllyn 0-4-2T design, this 5" gauge loco first appeared at Bentley in 2001. It had the honour of hauling the 100,000th ticket holder in September 2001. Like 'Sweet Pea', it is a powerful little engine, and usually appears on summer Saturday afternoons. A larger 7¼" model of the same loco is currently being built and we hope to see it in 2007.

Heavy haulers

Name	Type	Built	Gauge	Scale
EMMA APOLLO	0-4-2 Tank Freelance Tinkerbells. Steam	2002	7¼"	N/A

These two locos were first seen at Bentley in 2002. Built to the Tinkerbell design these enclosed-cab sister locos are expected to be seen regularly hauling passengers at Bentley throughout the summer seasons, usually in alternate years.

| **LADY HELEN** | Bo+2 Battery Electric | Pre 1984 Rebuilt 2005 | 7¼" | N/A |

This loco was rebuilt for 2005 having spent the previous 20 years out of use, its last run being at Bentley on our opening day back in 1985! Since its return it has seen service most weeks, also acting as a shuttle service during the winter.

| **BLACK SWAN** | 0-4-2 Tank Freelance "Thomas II". Steam | 1997 | 7¼" | N/A |

This locomotive appeared toward the end of 2006 season (named St. Elvan). It appeared at the Wood Fair Weekend, and is undergoing work to adapt to better suit the needs of Bentley Miniature Railway. It promises to be a powerful and useful hauler.

| **RACHEL, CRUNCHIE** | 4-wheel Petrol | Unknown | 7¼" | N/A |

These internal combustion locomotives are used for works trains, or occasionally as passenger standby on busy days.

Change here for a Walk in the Woods

Rolling Stock

Unlike locomotives, most rolling stock needs to be suited to full size passengers. The first passenger stock used for Bentley Miniature Railway was the scaled version Uckfield Flyer, previously employed on the portable track. Passengers sat on the roof of the vehicles, with their feet either side on footrests. Some miniature railways employ similar scale models of standard gauge coaches, however, BMR has developed two forms of dedicated passenger vehicle.

The first type is known as "sit astride" and was constructed for the early days, following the pattern of the Flyer. These are bogie vehicles with square bodies, 8 ft (2.4 m) long. Most of these run as single units, and have a hand brake. This applies the brake via a hydraulic system, as in a motor car, to one pair of axles, and the vehicles are often used singly with a battery loco for both driving and passengers. One pair has been combined as an articulated unit, with one bogie supporting the centre of the two cars. This, along with a few single units, has been fitted for vacuum braking; most locomotives have been likewise fitted for hauling multi-car trains. Each coach will take around 6 - 8 passengers, all facing forward.

The bodies of these coaches are demountable, and the frames may be used, with alternative box bodies, or alone, for carrying materials during maintenance and construction work.

The later type employs "sit-in" seats, and normally carries 4 passengers in two compartments with forward and backward facing seats. These are operated in sets of two coaches (two sets Club owned, and two private). Most are open, but roofed versions (privately owned) are being added.

Because the operating rules require any train of more than one passenger vehicle behind a locomotive (including tender or driving truck where appropriate) to have a Guard at the rear, several Guard's vehicles have been constructed. Of similar design to the sit-in coaches, they have only one pair of seats – one for the Guard, the second used for a "trainee" or other member of staff travelling, but more usually as storage of flags, whistle and ticket clippers, and particularly for the Guard's Tea or Coffee! As well as the open type, there is a closed Guard's Van, which is often used during the winter, with the Tram, as a Driving van, when in "shuttle" mode, whilst the track is blocked by engineering works.

In a typical train, the last vehicle will be a 4-wheel truck, used to carry passengers' luggage, pushchairs, etc. especially if they are alighting at Glyndebourne Wood. These were constructed by a member for his home railway, but are on long term loan.

The very latest sets of passenger vehicles are sit-in, similar to the second type, but of heavier construction. These were obtained during 2006. One set is privately owned, and the second by the Club. A set may be seen with St Elvan, in the picture on the rear cover, followed by the enclosed Guards van.

CHAPTER SIX

Signalling

In the earliest days, signalling and point operation was a manual job. In order to regulate the passage of trains between the Platform and Bypass roads, a person was positioned beside the Ridgewood Junction points (possibly not known by this name at first) and changed them by swinging over the weighted lever, then gave a 'Clear' flag to the train. Later, a pair of semaphore bracket signals was installed, still manually operated. At the trailing points at Ringmer Junction, trains simply ran over, setting the points as they passed. It is not clear when, but the trail-able locking mechanism (see Chapter 7) was removed from these trailing points only, to leave them totally un-worked to this day. In consequence, no trains may reverse over these. This system was fine when only one train was on the line; however, when a second train wanted to leave the platform whilst the first was on the circuit, a second signal person was allocated at the trailing points to signal trains over the junction. The drivers however had to keep a good lookout when following each other. The Author recalls, on probably his very first drive of a locomotive as a newcomer to the line, stalling on the gradient through lack of steam due to inexperience, and a following train coming within feet of running into the rear, through inattention, and requiring a "feet in the ballast" emergency stop! Such were the hazards of operation in those days – I hasten to add that the occasion was a Club private event, when no public passengers were present, and learners were permitted to drive. The need for a signalling system was therefore appreciated early. At first only the station facing points were motorised (in 1987), and a prototype junction colour light signal used to control trains over this. The signal was interlocked with the points, and power provided by portable batteries. Once the signal box was constructed, for the 1991 season, the point controls were relocated, and a simple station platform starter signal, plus an equivalent stop signal on the bypass were installed, to remove the need for the flagman. The signaling system has extended from the signal cabin since.

As mentioned in Chapter 7, the points were motorised by use of windscreen wiper motors, which produce linear motion from the rotation of a 12 V motor. Therefore, the points operation and control system is derived from 12 V battery systems. At each end of the stroke necessary to fully move the points, microswitches are used to send a signal to the control circuitry, and stop the motor, ready for it to be reversed to change the points back again. The batteries were initially kept charged by solar cells; however it was found that the cells would not keep up with the required charge, so, once mains power was made available in 1993, trickle chargers were installed. The batteries still provide the peak power required to move the points, and as backup for the signals in the event of loss of mains.

Although a semaphore signal was employed for the first manual signalling at Ridgewood Junction, when permanent signals were installed, these were of the colour light variety. These employ 12 V 5 watt vehicle (early) or 2.2 watt industrial (later) lamps, behind coloured lenses. The original lenses were of the type used in

Change here for a Walk in the Woods

Morris Minor motor cars, with the Green colour provided by lacquer inside the clear version. Subsequently standard industrial panel indicator lenses have been used. The signal heads are constructed from square plastic electrical trunking, and include the necessary relays to detect and switch the correct aspect. By default, if no relay is energised, a Red light will always show, thus failing safe if a wire breaks, or power fails (the operating rules instruct drivers to treat a signal showing no light as a Red indication). Most signals are of the 3-aspect type, showing (top to bottom) Green, Yellow, Red. A couple have a fourth, second Yellow aspect, above the Green. One 4-aspect signal is used at the top of the climb out of Glyndebourne Wood station (GW12) as the track between here and the tunnel entrance is divided into two short sections by GW14, and the area is on a curve that reduces visibility. The second 4-aspect signal is BC06, on the climb up to Horsted Sheds. Here, the driver needs to be informed whether to prepare to stop before the entrance to Bentley Central station, or whether the train is signalled around the bypass route. In the first case, BC10 will be at Danger, BC08 thus showing one Yellow, and BC06 showing 2 Yellows. If signalled through the bypass, BC12 will be Clear, and BC08 Green showing right-hand feathers, therefore BC06 will also show Green. The sequence of indications is described below in the section dealing with train detection, and automatic signal control. At facing junctions, a set of smaller white lights set at an angle, are placed at the top and one side of the head, to show the diverging route (generally the secondary one) the main route being indicated by a clear aspect with no white lights (known as "feathers" – the signal will not show feathers with a Red aspect).

The signals are mounted on small diameter rainwater pipe, at just above driver eye level, and are connected through a vehicle trailer plug and socket into local connection points, each wired into multicore cables leading to the relevant signal box.

Shunt and Subsidiary Signals

The main signals regulate the passage of trains in the "normal", clockwise direction, and have even numbers. Where it may be necessary to shunt a train in reverse, shunt signals are used, and these are numbered odd. They comprise three lights in a "vee on its side" formation. The light at the point of the vee normally shows White and one Red light shows horizontally to its left. When required to Clear for a shunting movement, the Red light is extinguished, and a second White is illuminated above it. This indicates to the driver that the route is set for the shunting movement, and he may reverse at caution, as far as any obstruction (e.g. if coupling onto a train), to the next main signal in the rear, or into the sheds as appropriate. Exceptions to this style are BC05, which controls access onto the Main Line at Ringmer Junction West from Ringmer Junction East, and BC07, giving access from Horsted Yard to the Turntable, Platform, or Bypass roads, with 3 sets of feathers to confirm which route is set. Both these are normal 3-aspect. BC11 and BC15 are normal design 2-aspect signals, showing Yellow or Red.

Early mechanical signalling employed at Ridgewood Junction, with 'REMUS' on a passenger service. Note the small section of track utilised for holding spare locos and coaches, as there were no sidings or turntable constructed by this time. It appears the tradition of spare staff congregating around the signaller started early! Wendy House stock storage in the background. Note also 3½" gauge rail.
August 1985.

The original level crossing and offloading area. A fence was soon erected to the left of the line. The crossing has now been replaced by plain track as part of the latest re-laying.
(Both - J Pollington)

Bentley Central Station
(A Morris)

Turntable and steaming bays

Signalling

Subsidiary indications are provided at the Signals controlling access to the Platforms, BC10 and GW04. These consist of two white lights set at 45 degrees, which light when the arrival platform is clear for a train to enter, but another train may be further along the platform. The associated main aspect will remain Red, to warn the driver to proceed with caution. The subsidiary indication at Bentley Central is controlled by the Platform Staff manually; at Glyndebourne Wood, the subsidiary indication is used only when Glyndebourne 'box is open for special events, and is controlled by the Signalman.

Train detection

The signalling system is designed to automatically set the signals to Red (Danger) behind a train, and to clear when the train passes the next signal. The Signalman may intervene to set any signal to Danger or, after confirming it is safe to do so, to clear a signal that has not cleared automatically due to failure of the detection system.

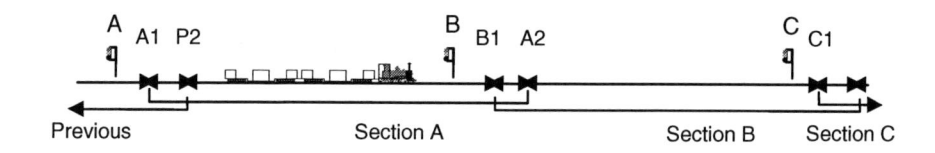

A "section" of track is defined as that length beyond (in advance of) a signal, until the next (stop) signal. Many railways, including the national railway system, detect the presence of any vehicle in a section by passing an electrical current along one rail, through a relay coil, and back to the other rail. Thus, the vehicle will cause the relay to de-energise, which is interpreted as an "occupied" indication. Whilst this would be possible on Bentley Miniature Railway, the method used here has treadles in the track. These are depressed by the flanges of a vehicle passing over them, opening or closing a switch contact to signify the entry to, or exit from, a section. The accompanying diagram shows the arrangement for three signals A, B, and C. A train is approaching Signal B, travelling left to right, Signal A is therefore showing Red. The Sections in advance of B and C are vacant, and these signals are therefore each showing Green. About 1 train length in advance of Signal B (not to scale) the train passes over treadle B1. This immediately sets Signal B to Danger. A further train length on, treadle A2 resets Signal A to Yellow (warning that 'B' is at Danger). Thus, even if the train were to stop immediately, any following train would be stopped at Signal B, well clear of the first. Having proceeded through Section B, the train passes Signal C. Treadle C1 sets Signal C to Danger. The following treadle B2 clears Signal B to Yellow, and Signal A to Green. If Signal A had the fourth aspect (second Yellow) the indication would be two Yellows, warning that B is showing one Yellow; Signal A would then only show Green once the train was clear of Section C.

Change here for a Walk in the Woods

The treadles do not alter the signals directly, but the operation of their switches is relayed to the relevant Signal Cabin. These actions are used to latch or release an electrical relay, one for each section. In accordance with common safety codes, when the relay is de-energised, the system considers the section to be occupied, thus ensuring any failure gives a Danger indication. The Section Relay drives a light situated in the signalling panel, which gives visual indication to the Signalman that a section is occupied. The same relay signals to the signalling logic the state of each section. The signalling logic controls the signals according to various conditions, for example, signals will not clear if trailing points are not set correctly for the route controlled by that signal, or will show the appropriate route for a facing junction; conversely, points may not be changed unless all signals applying to them are at Danger. The output of the logic determines whether the signal is set to Danger or Clear. A direct link between each signal and that in advance, determines whether the Clear indication is Yellow (next Signal at Danger) or Green (next Signal Clear). Junction signals are also linked with the points to determine which Signal in advance is relevant. Most signals may be selected, on the control panel, to either Automatic Control or held at Danger. In the former, the sequence of aspects will automatically follow that outlined above, as each train makes its way around the line. Additionally, certain signals, around stations and controlling junctions, may also be set to Semi-automatic. In Semi-automatic mode, signals return automatically to Danger, but will Clear only when the Signalman presses the appropriate pushbutton. This enables the signalman to hold the aspect to Danger when it is required to change a route. Generally, having brought a train onto the main line, the system is set to Automatic control, and a full time Signalman is not required. Bentley Central Platform Starter signal, BC16, is normally set to Semi-automatic control, with the Clear command being given from a button on the Platform, by the platform staff, just before the train is despatched.

As stated above, if the section relay is de-energised, the section is considered occupied, and the entry signal will remain at Danger. Occasionally, the actuation of the "exit" treadle does not cause the section relay to latch, either because of the failure of the exit treadle switch to close, or because the associated entry treadle switch remains open. In these cases, the Signalman may attempt to latch the section relay manually, or permit the Driver to pass a Danger signal at Caution, provided the Signalman is satisfied that the section is clear.

Because each section occupation relay is latched into the relevant state, the system "remembers" the last state. For example, the scenario described in Chapter 8, at Glyndebourne Wood, requires the following actions. The signals in Glyndebourne Wood station area, GW04 to 10 must be under Semi-automatic control.

When the stopping train enters the Platform, it sets the platform section relay to "occupied" thus holding GW04 at Danger. The Signalman holds the train at the Starter GW08, and changes both entry and exit points to the loop. Since this section is vacant, GW04 may be reset to Clear, and when the Loop Starter, GW10 is cleared, the following train passes through under Green signals. Once the through train has passed GW10, the Signalman may reset the both points to allow

Signalling

the stopping train to proceed. Because the Platform is still occupied, GW04 must be held at Danger, even if the Signalman should attempt to clear it. Similarly, although he may press the "Clear" button for GW08, the system knows that the section up to GW12 is still occupied, and will not clear. However, the request to Clear each signal is also held by the system, so as soon as the relevant section is vacated, the signal will Clear accordingly. This is used particularly at Bentley Central, when the request to release a second train soon after the first will hold BC16 at Danger, until the preceding train has passed BC18. The exception to "hold request to clear" is BC10 calling on lights, which are manually cleared by the signalman, or platform staff. The Author understands this function will be replaced by "approach control" for 2007.

Glyndebourne Wood

By the time the extension was opened, the signal system on the original circuit was complete, more or less as now found. For the opening of the route via Glyndebourne, the Bentley Central Starting Signal gave access to the extension, whilst the return was protected by a signal before Ringmer West junction. When on the extension, trains were controlled by a single signal at the foot of the cutting at Glyndebourne, hence only two trains could be on the extension at once. By the time of the 7¼" Gauge Society AGM in 1997, full signalling was installed, to allow as many locomotives on the track as possible at one time. Problems with the train detection system did mean a few delays, but the new arrangements coped well. For this event, the diamond crossing at Ringmer East was commissioned, to allow the visiting locomotives to be kept running continuously, whilst public trains operated from Bentley Central station.

Once the extension signalling system was under way, a signal box was erected at Glyndebourne Wood, and all signals and points from the Glyndebourne side of the level crossing were transferred to this box. The Glyndebourne Wood Signal Box obtains a mains supply at 110V, via a transformer in Bentley Signal Box and a cable alongside the track. Limited track occupation indications, and signal control, are relayed also to Bentley Signal Box from the Glyndebourne Wood area.

CHAPTER SEVEN

Trackwork and Civil Engineering

Original design

The initial circuit was designed to be level through the Station and by-pass loop, then climbing at the rear to a summit, before dropping back into the station. Clockwise running ensured that the ascending incline was gentler than the descent. The rail chosen for this first stage was light, of 1kg/metre; 18 mm high, 13 mm across the foot and 10 mm across the head, in nominal 10ft lengths. Wood sleepers of 1¼" square cross-section and 14" long were used, with the foot of the rail fastened using 2-off ¾" by No 8 screws plus 6mm washers under the heads. Each length of track required 27 sleepers (26 along the length, plus one under each joint shared with adjacent sections). Points (2 initially) were assembled from the same section rail, complete with the necessary crossings for three gauges – quite a feat of planning and engineering. The third point of this type was installed to access the Steaming Bays. As mentioned in Chapter 3, the original 7¼" and 5" gauge rails were soon joined by 3½" gauge, but this was little used, and the redundant rail was slowly removed, and recovered for spares and additions. When the access points to Horsted Yard sheds were made, only the larger two gauges were used.

This light construction has lasted 21 years, but requires frequent inspection and maintenance. During the spring of 2006, a programme to replace the old rail section was commenced, using the latest design of track (see below). The first section replaced this way was the bypass at Bentley Central, between the original points at Ridgewood Junction and the facing points at Ringmer East Junction.

Heavy construction

When the extension to Glyndebourne Wood was planned, experience drove the Railway to consider heavier construction. The rail section chosen was 3.76 lb/yard (1.87 kg/m) steel and in nominal 4 m lengths. This has dimensions of 26 mm high, 24 mm across the foot and 17 mm across the head. The rails were laid on sleepers 2" x 2" x 15" long. Twenty one sleepers are used per length. Rail fastenings were 10 gauge by 25mm flanged head self tapping screws.

The first requirement was to provide two entry and exit points for the new route in the light section. Initially, access to the extension was possible only from the Platform road; however, later the complex "scissors" crossing arrangement of Ringmer Junction East was completed, enabling trains from both Platform and Bypass to travel either toward Glyndebourne, or around the original circuit straight back to the Yard area. With the exception of the diamond crossing itself, which is welded from bar section on a steel plate, all this area was assembled in light section. The converter tracks from the old, light rail section, to the heavier were made by welding a short section of the 1 kg rail butted onto the heavier. The

Trackwork and Civil Engineering

transition from lighter to heavier construction was made 4 rail lengths from the Ringmer East junction trailing points on the 'outward' route, and one length from Ringmer West on the return.

Assembly of the new track panels was carried out at the Club's headquarters, in Uckfield some 3 miles from the Railway. Three rails per section were required. These were Common, 5", and 7¼". Straight sections went together quickly. For the curves, we had to work out: i) the nominal radius, ii) whether the common rail was inside or outside the curve, and iii) how many lengths would be required for the arc. The two inner lengths were then cut, and the three rails put through a rail bender ("curver" would be a better description, as a gentle curve was required). The benefit of such planning paid off when the track was laid, and very little adjustment was required. As track panels were completed, they were transported to the site, and carried out to be laid and ballasted, each section being 'made to order' as it were.

Immediately after leaving the original circuit, a bridge was constructed to cross the tail of a natural pond beside the line, which is fed by the stream running between the platform tracks and the bypass at Bentley Central. This area was developed by constructing a dam and installing pond liner to form an artificial pond that is kept full of water – even when the adjacent natural pond dries up in hot summers. The trailing exit points at Ringmer Junction (East) are sited on this bridge. Originally, the bridge was plain; however rustic wooden handrails were soon added, for safety when walking across. As the extension was constructed, works trains carried materials from the original circuit to the advancing railhead, and construction progressed generally clockwise around the new route. The final connection back into Ringmer West was achieved by Spring Bank Holiday 1995. To begin with, plain track was laid through Glyndebourne Wood bypass loop only. The first season was used to consolidate the track, with frequent re-packing and adjustment of alignment.

The first two points in the heavier construction were completed during Winter 1995/6, and installed to provide the platform at Glyndebourne Wood. Subsequently, the bay platform was added; this is used as a lay-by for stock at busy periods.

Changes

As the need arose to replace individual sleepers longer, 17", pre-treated ones were employed. These have been used particularly beneath joints, and especially on some of the curves, where gauge widening has occurred.

The whole of the curve around the Glyndebourne Wood cutting was re-sleepered during the winter 2005/6. Section by section, the track was lifted, every alternate old sleeper removed, and new 17" sleepers inserted and fastened with M6 x 25mm zinc plated flanged hex head screws with 20mm washers beneath the

Change here for a Walk in the Woods

head. Once the new sleepers were fastened and the rails gauged, the remaining original sleepers were replaced.

As mentioned above, at the beginning of 2006, new rail was purchased, of the heavier design. This was used with the 17" sleepers and M6 x 25mm fastenings to re-lay the Bentley Central bypass. After the end of the 2006 main season, and the October school half term running, the opportunity was taken to lift the old track around the top of the original circuit, between the Ringmer West Junction and Ridgewood Junction points. Ballast clearance commenced on 4 November 2006, preparatory to digging out the formation, helped by a digger, and renewing with fresh ballast, for replacement track to be assembled and laid. At the same time, the original spur line onto the turntable, including the access points, was removed, to enable the platform to be extended backward, thus allowing three full length trains to pull up in the platform. The remaining work for the 2006/7 winter includes relaying the platform road in new rail, and re-sleepering the remaining light section points.

Yard Tracks

Whilst the above styles of track are used everywhere on the main running lines, to save money, in the steaming bay area, and leading into the two Horsted Sheds, simple steel bar rails are used, generally welded onto steel strip cross pieces, which are then screwed onto wood sleepers. These sleepers are spaced more widely than the main line design. The design is a development of the original portable track used since the early days of the Club, and still in use for Model Railway Exhibitions and Fetes/Fairs etc.

In the steaming bays themselves, the bar track is raised on frames of sturdy "L" section, which are embedded in concrete. A swing-over section of similar design is used to load and offload locomotives and stock from road vehicles at the top of the loading ramp.

The original access to the bays via the turntable was from a facing point and short length of track, of small rail section, in the main line outside Bentley Central station. When Horsted Yard 1 shed was constructed, the trailing point giving access was also of small rail section, with an immediate transition to bar track as the line curved into the stub points (see below). It was soon realised that locomotive traffic from the steaming bays to the yard to collect stock, interfered with trains on the circuit. During the winter of 1997/8, a separate route was created, from a new access onto the turntable, and paralleling the main line. This was constructed in bar section, and the second set of points, to join the yard access points and form a crossover, were also constructed, in traditional fashion, from bar section. Both routes into the Yard were constructed in dual gauge, as far as the entry to the stub points. A 5" gauge loco could therefore travel from the steaming bay, to the spur, collect stock (7¼") and cross to the main line.

Trackwork and Civil Engineering

When Horsted Yard 2 shed was constructed, and the bar type track extended round adjacent to the main line, the spur was made into a set of layover points (below) with four routes, left to right – Horsted 2, Horsted 1 via stub points, and two additional routes into the right hand of Horsted 1 Shed. As mentioned elsewhere, the opportunity was finally taken to add a 5" gauge rail into the far right hand road, enabling the smaller stock to be stored under cover at last.

Points

The points on the main line have been constructed in matching style to the associated track. As noted, the main complication has been to include multiple gauges.

The drawing in Figure 7.1 (not to scale) shows a basic 7¼" gauge set of points, with the main components identified. The switch rails are joined by the stretcher and pivot from their respective heels, to fit against either stock rail. The stretcher is extended on one side to connect with the operating mechanism. The check rails guide the wheels through the gap formed by the wing rails and crossing.

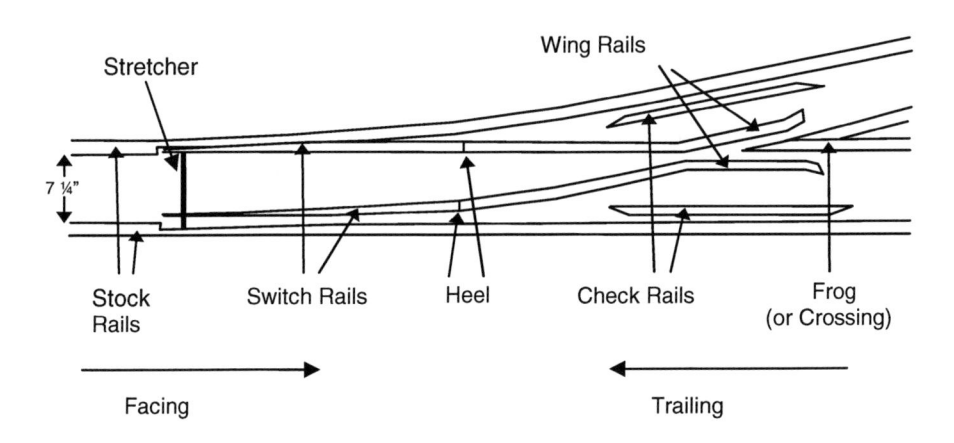

FIGURE 7.1

Figure 7.2 has superimposed in grey, plain lines representing the 5" gauge, measured from the Common Rail. Everywhere these lines cross another rail, a set of crossing, wing rails and check rails must be added. Note: because the thickness of the rails is exaggerated compared to the gauge, the spaces available are more than appears. The result of including 3½" gauge rails, in this case gauged from the 5" gauge rails, is shown in the picture on page 39, of the points leading to the turntable. The picture is historic since these points have been removed in the 2006/7 relaying in this area. Fortunately, once the first three triple gauge points were installed, the smallest gauge was abandoned, and the remaining points are only (!) dual gauge.

Change here for a Walk in the Woods

↑
Common Rail   FIGURE 7.2

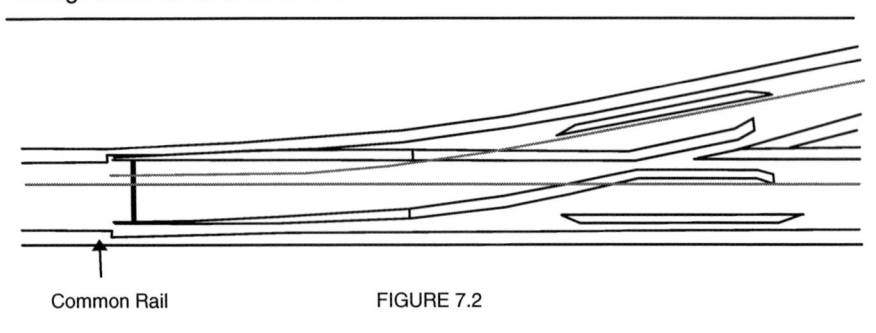

The original points, and indeed those used for the Club's portable track, have an ingenious locking arrangement, designed by a member at the time. This arrangement prevents the closed switch rail from being forced away from the associated stock rail, for example by the flange of a wheel passing through in the Facing direction; however, if a train approaches from the Trailing direction, against points set in the opposite direction (e.g. from the curved line in Figure 7.1), the flange pressure on the "free" switch rail releases the lock, and allows the wheel to pass between the closed switch and stock rails. Thus the points are held safe for trains in the facing direction, but will not be damaged by an inadvertent passage from the wrong trailing direction. We would not, however, generally trail through points set against a train.

The early operating mechanism was a weighted manual lever that moved an extension of the stretcher. As the signalling system became more complex, the points were mechanised, by use of electric motors from car windscreen wipers, producing a to and fro motion. Since motorising, the operating linkage has bypassed the trail-able function. However, by simply removing a short link between the motor and the point operating linkage, for example in the event of a motor failure, the turnout can be operated manually with the trail-able locking feature automatically re-engaged.

The more recent turnouts constructed for the Extension and for the Horsted-to-Turntable loco line do not have this trail-able mechanism. In this case the operating arm is sprung in both directions to ensure the switch rails are positively located against the stock rails, again allowing trailing without damage, but not generally used as such.

Layover and Stub Points

These points have been constructed, for simplicity and reduced cost, from bar section, to be used in areas away from the passenger carrying main lines.

Five-way stub points in foreground, layover points beyond leading to Horsted 1 (left hand 3 roads) and Horsted 2 (right hand road) sheds.

A last view of the triple-gauge points giving access to the turntable from the main line. These have now been removed in the track re-laying.

Construction of the Trackbed for Glyndebourne Wood Platform road
– October 1995 (J Pollington)

Looking from the top right of the above picture, 2006. Platform line to left and bay
to right. Could the latter become the return line from the Wildfowl extension?

Trackwork and Civil Engineering

The first style of layover points was used during a visit of the 7¼" Gauge Society for their AGM in 1997. Temporary tracks, using the Club's portable track sections, (7¼" gauge only) were laid into marquees in the centre of the original circle. These layover points lie on top and between the normal track, in order to divert stock on and off. Once the manoeuvre was complete, the points were moved to one side to allow normal traffic to pass. A similar system was used on the narrow gauge Tal-y-llyn Railway in Wales, circa the 1970's, to give access to an area for tipping ash etc. This became known as the "sliding siding"! This method will come back into use at BMR for some temporary sidings, off of the bypass line.

With the opening of Horsted Yard 1 shed, which has five roads, it was necessary to bring the five roads into one in a short distance. To do this, we produced five-way points. Rather than make 5 sets of switch blades, which would have been complicated, a design was produced, with a single pair of flexible rails, which can be moved laterally to align with one of five routes. The remainder of the points was constructed traditionally, with welded frogs (crossings) and checkrails. These points are operated by a wheel, driving an arm via threaded gear, thence moving the stretcher to any required position. The photo on page 39 shows the 5-way points, viewed from the sheds, with the dual gauge layover points beyond.

These layover points are picked up at the free end, and moved manually to align with one of the roads. For this reason, the rails are not welded solidly to cross pieces, but to "L" sections which are in turn free to pivot on the wooden sleepers. Welded fishplates outside the fixed tracks locate the ends laterally. Further examples, but in 7¼" gauge only, are used outside Horsted 2 shed.

Trackbed

Before track can be laid, a suitable foundation must be provided. Whether level with the surroundings, on an embankment, or in a cutting, the track bed is provided by excavating into the ground about 6" (150 mm) deep, and 2' 6" (760 mm) wide along the route. This strip is bordered by concrete strips, cast in situ on edge, to hold back the surrounding earth. See the photograph opposite. At the bottom of the excavations, a membrane is laid to hold back the earth (and to some extent the weeds) from mixing with the ballast. Originally, this membrane was provided by redundant stout plastic bags, (free!) pierced to allow water to drain away. Recently, and for the reconstruction of the original circuit, geotextile has been employed, at greater cost, but more effective. A layer of ballast is laid on this membrane; various types of sub-ballast have been used, including scrapings from road re-surfacing. The latest is, however, of quality stone. The track panels are laid on the sub-base, and levelled, before further ballast is added between and around the sleepers to hold the track in place. On certain sharper curves, wood blocks have been inserted between selected sleepers and the concrete edging, to assist with preventing movement.

CHAPTER EIGHT

A Trip around the Railway, Operation and Tickets

Bentley Central

Passengers access the departure platform by passing to the left of the station building. On busy days, the ticket office window is manned, and the card tickets sold before the passenger approaches the platform; however, when operated by a minimum staff, paper tickets are sold from an old 'bus conductor's ticket machine on the platform. The platform staff will not permit the public to enter the platform until their train is ready and stationary, thus promoting safety.

A typical train will comprise the locomotive (steam we hope!) with two carriages each holding 4 persons. Behind these, a short bogie vehicle provides for the Guard, and at the end of the train, a 4-wheel wagon, which carries push-chairs, backpacks, etc. for passengers alighting at Glyndebourne Wood for a walk. At the front end of the platform are situated a water tower for loco water, and coal facilities. There is also a gate leading to the bypass area, for staff access only.

Out to Glyndebourne

Trains travel clockwise round the route, thus providing left hand running on the double track section. Once ready to depart, the driver, or platform staff when available, presses the Train Ready to Start button. If the signalman has set the system to "remote" this action will clear the starting signal (BC 16) to Green. This signal is sited just before the junction, and is a three aspect colour light type, with "feathers" to indicate the diverging route around the original circle. When the signal clears, our driver opens the regulator, and we are off. Taking the left road at the junction, we enter the extension itself and cross the bridge over the pond. Once round the 60 ft radius curve, the train accelerates along the first straight, encountering signal BC18. Shortly before the right-hand curve, we come alongside the return track, and the double track begins. The first hundred metre distance post is encountered just after the bend, and the long straight run commences. About half way up the straight, a level crossing is sited, which provides access to the field on our right, and is protected on the approach by signal BC20. The crossing is not normally used, except on special events at Bentley Wildfowl. When the crossing is in use, signal BC20 is set to semi-automatic control, and staff stationed at the crossing to open and close the gates. Only when the gates are opened to trains will the signal (and its equivalent GW20 in the opposite direction) be cleared manually. On most days, this signal like the majority is automatic. Trains are required to whistle for the crossing, especially since the hedge to our left has grown up, reducing visibility in this direction. The line has been nominally level from the station to this point, but now a 1 in 350 up grade begins, so the

A Trip around the Railway

driver puts on a little more steam. We have passed from control of Bentley Central to Glyndebourne Wood signal box, and the next signal, GW02 is sited about half way between crossing and the entrance to Glyndebourne Wood Station. At the end of the straight, we pass the 200 metre post. As we are to stop at Glyndebourne Wood Station, the junction signal (GW04) shows a Yellow aspect, and left route feathers. Steam is shut off, and we take the straight ahead route across the points. The gradient levels off for the station. Our train coasts to a halt at the platform, and passengers may embark, disembark, or remain on board as they wish. To our left, a bay platform road is to be seen. Although not normally used for passenger services, trains may lay over here; faulty stock may be left out of service; or a works train wait whilst maintenance is carried out.

To the Summit

As this is a busy day, the Platform starter has been set at Red, but on most days, the 'box is unmanned, and all Glyndebourne signals are automatic. If we look back, we see a further train approaching. This is signalled through on the main line, and runs past with a whistle. We watch it forge up the cutting, until it passes the next signal, whereupon, the signalman resets the road for us, and clears our starter (GW08) to Yellow. Immediately after joining the main line again, the gradient is 1 in 150, and the locomotive begins to work hard, especially from a standing start. The return track leaves our side, and the cutting commences, so we are on single track for a while. At the end of the straight, the 300 metre post, Whistle board, and signal GW 12 are encountered in quick succession. This signal is 4-aspect, and protects the run around the blind cutting to the tunnel. The train we are following, having had a run at the hill, is now well ahead, so the signal is showing 2 Yellows for our train. Our driver obeys the whistle instruction, as visibility is limited on the 60 ft radius curve, and there may be workers on the track. A short way into the curve, the gradient changes from 1 in 150 up to 1 in 350 down, and we begin to coast for a time. Toward the end of the curve, signal GW14 shows Yellow, then Green, and once round the curve, and on to the straight, speed may be increased again, as the tunnel looms ahead. Signal GW16 at the entry to the tunnel changes from Yellow to Green as we approach. We pass through the tunnel, which permits access to the centre of the loop, with a whistle, and our younger passengers yell and scream. The far portal marks 400 metres from Bentley Central.

Back home

At the exit from the cutting, the track levels out, and becomes double once more, as we pass Glyndebourne Wood in the opposite direction. There is no platform for this direction, so our train continues round the left-hand bend. A further signal (GW18) at the end of the curve breaks up the section, and we run on Yellow lights down the straight, and to the level crossing. Midway between Glyndebourne and the crossing is the 500 metre mark. Signal GW20, before the crossing, marks the end of the Glyndebourne signalling area. On to the level once again, we slow

Change here for a Walk in the Woods

down, so as not to catch the preceding train, and the first signal back into Bentley control (BC02) just before the exit curve, clears as we reach it.

As our track diverges from the outward line, we pass the 600 metre post, and soon the line begins to climb at 1 in 130, approaching the trailing junction with the original route. The locomotive whistles for the junction signal BC04, which is cleared for us. Once over the junction points, there is a short bend to the right, and the gradient steepens to 1 in 100. A good head of steam is required to surmount this, but our driver has all in control. We rumble over the concreted level crossing (now removed) and pass signal BC06 and the 700 metre post. BC06 is another 4-aspect version, giving advance warning of the state of the signal controlling entry to the station; this would normally be showing 2 Yellows, but this time shows a single Yellow, and signal BC08 by the carriage sheds warns us to stop. The signalman has decided to route the previous train around the by-pass and back onto the main line. Once this train has passed BC12, the signalman resets the route for us and junction signal gives a Yellow for the straight route. The gradient has changed from 1 in 100 up to the same grade down, so when the signal clears we restart with no problem. Just beyond the facing junction, we are back on level track again. Signal BC10 shows Red, but with two diagonal white lights permitting entrance to the arrival platform under caution. We have completed about 760 metres. Once the passengers get off, we can pull forward to the departure platform, ready to start again.

The section of route between Ringmer East and Ringmer West junctions is used only occasionally nowadays, normally to enable a light locomotive to run around from the platform (or bypass) to the sheds.

Timetable and Staffing

Bentley Miniature Railway does not operate to a strict timetable. However, each year a Timetable Leaflet is published, announcing the operating days. On busy Sundays and Bank Holidays, the first train will run from 10:30 – 11:00 a.m. provided passengers require it. Saturdays are more leisurely, starting around lunch time, although if a few members arrive early, trains may start sooner. Generally, staffing on weekends and Bank Holidays is not a problem.

The mid-week operations depend on availability of staff. A minimum of two members are required to operate the Railway. At least one must be competent to take charge for the day, as "Track Marshall". Provided the second member is able to carry out at least one of the duties as Driver, or Platform and Ticket sales, the Tram locomotive, plus single carriage, can be put into operation. This train may be operated under the rules by a single person. The second person remains on the Platform, to greet potential passengers, and to sell travel Tickets, which is normally carried out once passengers are on board. Both train and platform will have available one of the Railway's private radios, which enable the train crew to summon assistance if necessary (fortunately this is extremely rare!) or the station staff to communicate with the driver. There is a contingency for the Track Marshall

A Trip around the Railway

to operate the Railway alone, using the Bentley Wildfowl radio system to obtain assistance. To the best of the author's knowledge, this has never been required; although he came close to invoking this on one occasion when the second member failed to turn up, and a hurried substitution was made! Because of the importance of having enough staff for midweek running, a roster is operated to ensure at least one Track Marshall and one other member are on site per day.

The Track Marshall's day starts with unlocking the Station and Signal box, and signing into the day's sheet for Club insurance purposes. Either he or another qualified member will carry out the morning's track inspection, normally by foot, although a cautious drive round with a train may be made. The inspection looks for obstructions on the track, particularly in the flangeways. Overhanging or fallen branches around the cutting may also be a problem. The resident rabbit population enjoy nothing better than to dig up the ballast, and spread it over the rails! (Well, there may be one thing they prefer...) so a broom is taken on the inspection, to replace the diggings, and restore the route. The opportunity should also be taken to check that no rail joints have come apart, and no other problems are evident. The inspector will then sign off the track as safe for operations. If a train was not used for the inspection, the next move is to set the points in order to bring the first train from the shed. Invariably this will be the Tram, and once she is in the Platform, the points may be reset for the main line, and the signals left in Automatic mode (see Chapter 6). A quick check of the ticket float, and confirmation that the previous day's booking clerk has entered the correct ticket numbers on the day's sheet, and we are almost ready to open to the public.

Three signboards are put out, two adjacent to the departure platform entrance: the BENTLEY CENTRAL nameboard, and an information board including details of the day's locomotive(s). The third board is placed at the top of the footpath from the Bentley entrance directing the Public to the Railway. Placing of these boards accompanies unlocking of entrance and exit gates (and usually a visit to the toilets in the main complex!) and signifies the Railway is open for business. Sharing out of these, and the rest of the day's duties, is by mutual agreement, and often depends on the experience of the members involved. However, the Track Marshall needs to be able to do any or all of these duties, amongst others.

Although the Railway can be, and often is, run with a skeleton staff of 2, the use of the Tram limits the number of passengers per train to 6 (plus babes in arms). On a busy day, this could result in long queues at the platform. Fortunately, days that attract extra passengers also attract more members, whether rostered, or ad-hoc. With a third member, a train of two coaches may be put into service, with Driver, Guard and Platform staff. Normally this would use a battery electric 'diesel outline' locomotive; however, with a suitable selection of staff, one member may be released to fire up one of the steam locomotives. Four or more members on site is probably the ideal for steam operation. With the exception of the Club's Tram, battery electric Hymec, and Steam loco HERCULES, locomotives belong to members, and are operated only by their owners – although other suitably qualified members may drive with the owner's permission. Whilst steam is raised, the other members maintain the service with the Tram. Subsequent additional

Change here for a Walk in the Woods

members on any day will permit putting other trains into service, if required, or rotation of duties, giving opportunities for rest, or to carry out maintenance or projects around the Railway. At busy periods, two platform staff operate, one to despatch trains, and the other to assist the passengers alighting at the opposite end of the platform. Only if there is sufficient staff is the Booking Office opened, selling card tickets through the window, and relieving the platform staff of one duty.

The route is just under ½ mile (800 m) round, and the permitted speed is 5 mph (8 km/h) giving a non-stop time of around 6 minutes per trip. Allowing for a short halt at Glyndebourne Wood, a train will arrive back at Bentley Central about 6½ to 7 minutes after departure. By the time the passengers have alighted, the train has moved forward to the departure platform, and the new passengers boarded, the next trip will depart 10 minutes after the previous one. This is borne out by the author's log book of journeys with his own locomotive. It may be possible to cut this time to 9 minutes occasionally, but this would not be sustainable over a long period. Putting on a second train makes 5 minute intervals possible. A third set may only reduce the interval to 4 minutes, but provides slightly longer rests between journeys for each locomotive – important when it is necessary to take on coal and water, or to oil round the motion! This way, in theory one train will be half way around the circuit, as one departs, and the third arrives. Of course, such short intervals are only sustained as long as passengers are waiting for a ride. Once the queue disappears, three trains may end up in the platform at once, which is just possible with the length of platform and trains. Although when there is a continuous queue of passengers, a fourth train may be coped with, if the demand reduces, the extra train becomes an embarrassment, requiring the front train to leave empty, or meaning the last train is held outside the platform, which does not go down well with its passengers! Nonetheless, on busy days, additional trains may be seen, often operating via the bypass line, for example as demonstration goods trains, or for testing locomotives.

Part of the purpose of the Railway is to take visitors from Bentley Central to Glyndebourne Wood, to permit them to take a 'Walk in the Woods'. Most tickets are sold as "Returns", allowing the passenger to return from Glyndebourne Wood on a later service. However "Singles" are available should anyone choose to travel one way, and walk back. Since all trains operate from Bentley Central, and do not remain at Glyndebourne Wood, when the passengers wish to return they must summon a train, by pressing a button that sounds a buzzer at Bentley. The challenge for the platform staff is then to send an empty train to Glyndebourne Wood as soon as possible, or to ensure that passengers intend to alight, thus allowing the returning ones to board. When the queue extends down the platform approach slope, and past the station building, it is a hard decision to decline to admit the next group of passengers!

The busiest period for the Railway is Bentley's Wood Fair Weekend in September. This runs from Friday to Sunday. On the Friday, the normal pattern of operation is followed, but with the maximum number of trains in service. However, on Saturday and Sunday a different service operates. As many as 8 trains may be in service,

The 'Last Spike' – joining up the Extension May 1995
(J Pollington)

Bentley Signal Cabin and Arrival platform

A selection of tickets from the collection of John Pollington (approximately full size). Note that early tickets were printed two-coloured and double sided. Later are single sided. Current versions are in the top row. 1996 was the first year of the full title for the Railway.

and 4 will be allocated to Bentley Central, returning non-stop, via the loop at Glyndebourne Wood. Similarly, the remaining trains operate from Glyndebourne Wood, non-stop via Bentley Central bypass. Signalmen work at both Bentley Central and Glyndebourne Wood 'boxes, regulating the trains, and ensuring they take the correct routes! Glyndebourne Wood platform is manned, with at least 2 staff. When not rostered to drive for the Saturday of Wood Fair, the author is often allocated to Glyndebourne Wood platform, and in 2006 was part of the team that sold more tickets in the day than Bentley Central, a feat repeated by the Sunday Team also!

At times, a day on Bentley Miniature Railway can be exhausting, other days, when the weather is poor and few passengers present themselves are less enjoyable. However, it is always rewarding, and an opportunity to "play trains". The variety of passengers, and the changing seasons mean that one journey is never exactly the same as another.

Tickets and Fares

Initially, cinema-style plain numbered ticket rolls were used. Subsequently, card railway-type tickets were purchased. Issued from the Booking Office window, these are stamped by a redundant British Railways date machine. Two types, Green and White are now used, each with their own serial ranges. The different types have been used to denote, variously, White for Full and Coloured for Special fares; since the use of Glyndebourne Wood station, White are now Return, and Green Singles or Specials. The fares for 2006 were set at 60p Return and 40p Single. Adults pay the same fare as Children.

With the increase in mid-week operations, carried out with skeleton staff, a redundant 'bus type paper ticket machine was obtained. This issues tear-off paper tickets, from rolls within the machine, and, as stated above, enables tickets to be sold on the Platform. The same colours and denominations as above are used.

Conclusion

I hope you have enjoyed our wander through the history and operation of Bentley Miniature Railway. If you bought this book after a visit to the line, I trust you have found the visit behind the scenes interesting, and will come again; if you are yet to visit us, I hope you have been encouraged to do so. Either way, we look forward to seeing you soon, and you will be assured of a welcome.

Change here for a Walk in the Woods

Acknowledgements

Inevitably, when writing about a club project, it is difficult to avoid speaking of personalities. There have been many people involved in various ways over 21 years, and before with the origins of UMRC. However, I am unable to mention every one involved, so have avoided using any names. I apologise to any of my fellow members if their contributions have not been acknowledged; be sure, BMR could not have been brought to its current state without you!

Much help in producing this book has been provided by other members of Uckfield Model Railway Club. In particular, I am grateful to Alan Morris (BMR Webmaster) for use of text from the web-site. John Pollington has given assistance with proof reading, but particularly has corrected the Chapter on Signalling. Parts of the text referring to the early days of BMR have been adapted from an article by the Author in a society magazine, itself based on articles for other magazines, by other Club members.

Details of the Bentley Wildfowl and Motor Museum site have been gleaned from their publications, and website, and I acknowledge the use of this information, and the help of the current site manager, Barry Sutherland, in the Chapter outlining the history of Bentley House.

Contacts

For further details the reader is advised to contact:

Uckfield Model Railway Club Ltd

www.uckfieldmrc.co.uk

Club Secretary: **Steve Rowley** Wynders Cottage, Barnetts Hill, Peasmarsh, Rye, East Sussex. TN31 6YJ Telephone: 01797 230521

Bentley Miniature Railway

www.bentleyrailway.co.uk
Email: enquiries@bentleyrailway.co.uk

Bentley Wildfowl and Motor Museum, Halland, Near Lewes, East Sussex, BN8 5AF.

Tel: 01825 840573/841451 Fax: 01825 841322
Email: barrysutherland@pavilion.co.uk. Website: www.bentley.org.uk